CHILDREN'S REFERENCE

ANCIENT & MEDIEVAL HISTORY

Capella

This edition published in 2008 by Arcturus Publishing Limited
26/27 Bickels Yard, 151–153 Bermondsey Street,
London SE1 3HA

ISBN: 978-1-84193-823-3

Designers: Q2A India and Talking Design
Editors: Rebecca Gerlings and Alex Woolf

Printed in China

Contents

Introduction

Ancient history begins with the invention of writing by the Sumerians approximately five thousand years ago and ends with the fall of the Western Roman Empire in about 476 AD. Medieval History takes up the story from this point and finishes in approximately 1500. During this six and a half thousand year period, human progress was dramatic. Primitive farming communities developed into powerful and warlike civilizations. Humans developed the technologies to build vast structures and the artistic talents to create objects of lasting beauty. Besides the classical civilizations of Europe, rich cultures also developed in the Americas and in Asia. In the Middle Ages, in Christian Europe and the Islamic empires of North Africa and Asia, religion became both the major inspiration for art and culture and a driving force for military conquest.

In this book, you will discover many fascinating facts about human history during the ancient and medieval periods. Do you know, for example, which ancient civilization invented the first calendar? Or what ancient wall is over 4,039 miles (6,500 km) long? What was the Hundred Years War all about, and who fought it? And what ancient South American city was so well hidden that it remained undiscovered by the outside world until the 20th century? You can find out the answers to these questions and many more in the pages of this book.

Ancient Mesopotamia and Egypt

Mesopotamia and Egypt are two of the world's oldest human civilizations. The Mesopotamian civilization was located in the area between the Tigris and Euphrates Rivers in Southwest Asia. This is the area of modern-day Iraq, Syria, and Turkey. The Egyptian civilization grew along the banks of the Nile River in North Africa. The Egyptian and the Mesopotamian civilizations were both river valley cultures. They developed and flourished because of the clever ways in which they used their rivers.

▲ Location of the ancient civilizations of Egypt and Mesopotamia.

Key facts:

- The ancient Mesopotamians invented the first calendar. Their calendar was based on the movement of the Sun and Moon. The calendar had 12 months, except every fourth year, which had 13 months.
- The Sumerians invented the wheel. They made carts and wagons to transport people and goods. They also used the wheel to make pottery.
- Ancient Egyptians believed in life after death. According to them, the soul of the dead person traveled to another world and another life. This is why they buried food, clothes, and everything else that a person would need, along with the dead body.
- The gods and goddesses of the ancient Egyptians and Mesopotamians were part-human and part-animal forms. These deities represented various natural elements like the Sun, Moon, heaven, sky, and water. They also had gods of love, war, protection, childbirth, agriculture, and magic.

The Mesopotamian civilization began around 5000 BC, when people began to learn how to grow crops and to live as a community. These early people, called the Sumerians, learned to use water from the Tigris and the Euphrates by making canals, dykes, and tanks. They watered the hot and dry land to grow grain for food, such as wheat, chickpeas, and barley. They also began rearing domestic animals such as cattle, fowl, and dogs. As the civilization grew and thrived, small city-states were formed, each with its own fortress. The Sumerians traded with the Persians and the Indus Valley people. They made pottery, carved metal objects, stone sculptures, and mud-brick buildings. They also began weaving cloth with linen fiber. They even invented cuneiform, an early written language.

▼ Carvings on clay
The word 'cuneiform' has been derived from the Latin word *cuneus*, meaning wedge. Ancient Mesopotamians used a reed or any sharp tool to write on clay tablets, giving this ancient script its name.

Around 2000 BC, the Sumerians were defeated by the Akkadians, who made Babylon their capital and began ruling southern Mesopotamia. Hammurabi was the most powerful Babylonian king. He brought the entire area of Mesopotamia under his rule. By 1350 BC, the Assyrians became powerful in the north. King Sargon spread Assyrian rule over all of Mesopotamia, right up to Thebes in Egypt. The Mesopotamian civilization ended in 539 BC, when the Persians took control of Babylon.

▸ Farming in ancient Egypt
Ancient Egyptians mainly cultivated wheat, barley, flax, fruit, and vegetables. The agricultural season lasted for about nine months. Farming stopped from July to November during the annual flooding of the Nile.

Egyptian civilization

Farming communities began developing in the areas by the Nile River around the 11th century BC. Like the Mesopotamians, the Egyptians also built canals and waterways and made tools like the plough to help them grow grain for food. By 3000 BC, the first Egyptian kingdom was formed. The king was called a 'pharaoh' and Egyptians believed that their pharaohs were gods on Earth.

Enterprising Egyptians

The Egyptians invented a kind of paper from the stem of the papyrus plant. They also invented hieroglyphics, another early written language. Early Egyptian buildings were made of mud bricks, but later palaces, temples, and pyramids were made with huge stone blocks. The most impressive structures are their temples and pyramids that contain the tombs of Egyptian pharaohs and queens. The royalty were mummified and buried along with food, fine clothes, jewelry, furniture, and even servants, ready for the afterlife.

▲ **Tribute to the Sungod**
The Temple at Luxor is a typical example of Egyptian architecture.

The ancient Egyptians were very religious people. They were also equally artistic, so it was not surprising that they decorated their buildings with paintings and sculptures of their gods and kings. They also learned to spin and weave cotton and mastered the art of glass making. The Egyptian civilization lasted for more than 3,000 years, until Alexander the Great, the king of Macedonia, invaded Egypt and defeated the Egyptians.

Try these too:

Ancient India and China (p 10–11),
Ancient Architecture (p 16–17),
Medieval Asia (p 22–23)

Ziggurats and pyramids

The ziggurats of Mesopotamia and the pyramids of Egypt are the most outstanding structures of these two civilizations. Ziggurats (see below) are huge, stepped structures that serve as a platforms for temples. Early pyramids looked similar to ziggurats, except they were hollow inside and contained tombs. The most famous pyramids in Egypt are the Great Pyramids at Giza, near Cairo.

Ancient India and China

The Indus Valley civilization in India and the ancient Chinese civilization are the two oldest river valley cultures in the eastern hemisphere. The Indus Valley civilization, also known as the Harappan civilization, developed on the banks of the Indus and Ghaggar-Hakra Rivers. It was spread over present-day Pakistan, western India, and parts of Afghanistan. The Chinese civilization began along the banks of the Yangtze River in central China.

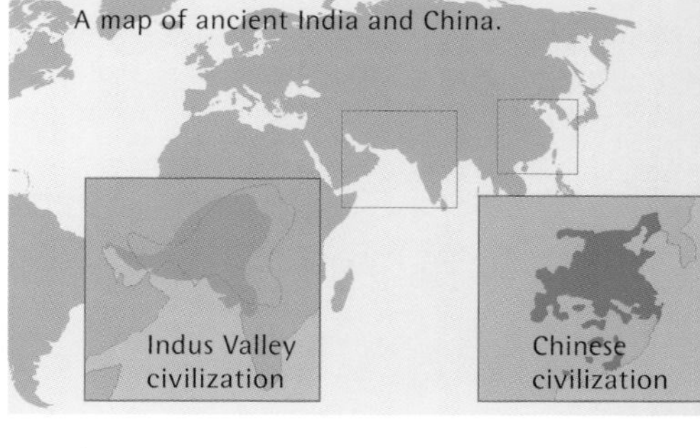

A map of ancient India and China.

▲ An architectural marvel
The Great Bath at Mohenjodaro was probably the first public water tank or swimming pool. The tank was lined with closely laid plastered brick. A layer of tar was also applied on the floor and the sides of the tank to prevent it from leaking.

▼ Metal works
The Harappans were skilled craftsmen. They had great knowledge about metals as is evident from these household and farming tools made from copper.

The Indus Valley civilization developed at the about the same time as the civilizations of Mesopotamia and Egypt. The Indus Valley civilization was spread over a larger area than the other ancient cultures. The first farming communities in this area existed in 6500 BC. However, it was only around 4000 BC that the first signs of the Indus culture were seen at Harappa, one of the biggest Indus cities. Other important sites of the Indus culture are Mohenjodaro and Lothal. The Indus people grew a number of crops including wheat, rice, and cotton. They also reared domestic animals. Their towns were well planned and had buildings made of mud bricks. All houses had bathrooms, and the waste water flowed into closed drains that lined the streets. The Indus people also built large structures such as dockyards and granaries (to store grain).

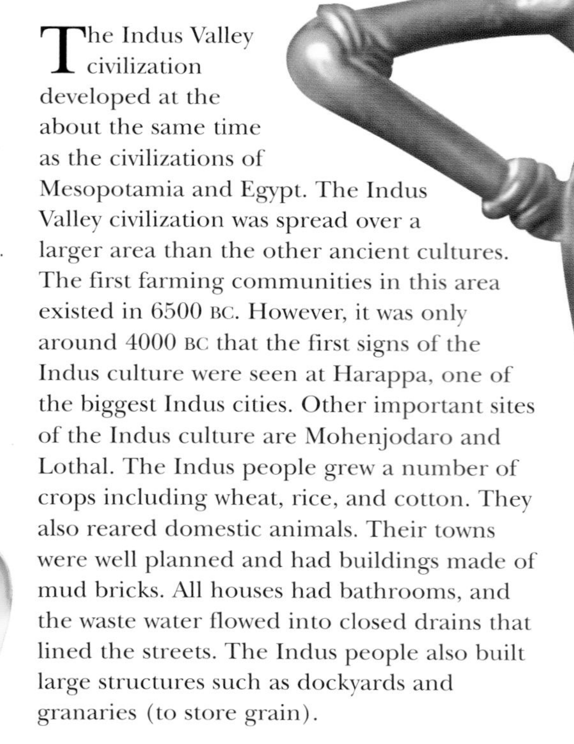

▶ Works of art
The Harappans made fine jewelry, terracotta figurines, and bronze sculptures. This 4,500-year-old bronze figurine of a dancing girl is a fine example of Harappan art.

The Harappans built ships and were believed to have traveled to Mesopotamia and Persia. They made fine jewelry and terracotta figurines. Like the Egyptians and Mesopotamians, the Harappans also developed a pictorial written language. By 1800 BC, the Indus Valley villages were abandoned, probably due to invasions by Aryans from the north. The Indus Valley civilization was followed by the Vedic period. At this time, Hinduism become a major religion and the main religious texts, the *Vedas, Brahmanas* and *Upanishads,* were written. By 600 BC, the northern part of the country was divided into 16 kingdoms and the society was divided into four castes: the *Brahmins,* or priests, the *Kshatriyas,* or warriors, the *Vaishyas,* or merchants and the *Shudras,* or laborers.

Great Wall of China

The Great Wall of China is a series of massive stone and mud fortifications that stretch across the northern border of China. The earliest walls were built in the third century BC to protect China from Mongolian and Manchurian invasions. Later, during the Qin dynasty, the wall was made bigger. Work on the wall continued until the 16th century AD, under various dynasties. A large part of the wall that we see today was built during the rule of the Ming dynasty. It is now over 4,039 miles (6,500 kilometers) long and at its highest point it is about 25 feet (7.6 meters) high.

Ancient China

Several farming villages had formed in various parts of China by 5000 BC. These villages grew in size and developed their own pottery, culpture, and architectural styles, and over the years exchanged ideas and techniques. In 2000 BC, all these scattered settlements came together under a single ruler.

Dynasties of ancient China

Ancient China was ruled by a series of dynasties, starting with the Xia dynasty. The Xia was followed by the Shang dynasty. During this period, the Chinese written language and the art of casting bronze vessels developed. During the Zhou dynasty, iron was introduced into China. The government controlled agriculture and stored away all the surplus crops. In 221 BC, the Qin dynasty came to power. Emperor Qin Shi Huangdi unified China as a single country under his rule. He decreed that a common language (the Qin language) be used all over the kingdom. A written language with over 3,000 characters was invented and the calligraphic style of writing began developing. Coins were also introduced. After Huangdi's death, the Qin dynasty lost power and the kingdom broke up into many parts.

Chinese silk
Around 3000 BC, the Chinese learned to make silk thread from cocoons. They wove very delicate silks and painted on them.

The stone of heaven
Jade represented nobility, perfection, constancy and immortality. The Chinese saw it as a link between man and god.

Key facts:

- Confucius was a great Chinese philosopher who lived in the 5th century BC. Confucianism is a religious, political, and moral school of thought taught by him. His teachings have been collected in a book called *Analects of Confucius*.
- The ancient civilizations of China, India, Egypt, and Mesopotamia were connected by the Silk Road. This land route stretched from China to Turkey and was used to trade in goods such as gold, silk, porcelain, and jewelry.
- The written language of Harappans was made up of at least 400 symbols. However, unlike Egyptian hieroglyphics, the Indus script has still not been deciphered. This is because there are no books or carved passages in the Indus script. The only evidence of this language is on terracotta seals, which have only 4 to 5 symbols each.

Try these too:

Ancient Mesopotamia and Egypt (p 8–9), Ancient Architecture (p 16–17)
The Age of Exploration (p 134–135)

Ancient Greece

The ancient Greek civilization is considered to be the beginning of all Western civilizations. It was based not just in mainland Greece, but also on several small islands in the Aegean Sea, in Cyprus, along the Aegean coast of Turkey, in Sicily, and in certain parts of Italy. Ancient Greek settlements were also located in places as far as Ukraine (in present-day Russia), Libya (in Southwest Asia), Romania, and even Egypt.

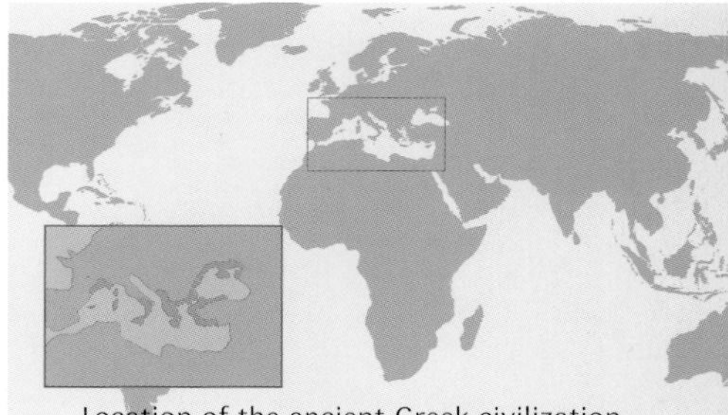

Location of the ancient Greek civilization.

Key facts:

- Ancient Greeks made pottery for their daily use in a variety of shapes. Some of the most common shapes were the amphora (wine jars), hydria (water jars), and krater (mixing bowls). These vessels were painted with geometric designs or human figures hunting or engaged in battle. Some depicted scenes from Greek mythology.
- In ancient Athens, only men had the right to vote or be elected to the government. Women were not sent to school. They were trained in housework and married by the time they were 13.
- Coins were introduced around 600 BC. The first coins were just lumps of gold or silver. Later, flat discs with figures of gods or goddesses, faces of kings, or even messages, were made.
- By 338 BC, most of Greece was under the control of the neighboring kingdom of Macedonia. The death of Alexander the Great, king of Macedonia, in 323 BC marked the end of ancient Greek civilization.

Long before the ancient Greek civilization developed, other smaller, yet well-developed, cultures flourished in the Aegean islands and on the Greek mainland. The earliest of these was the Minoan civilization, which began around 3000 BC, on the island of Crete. Knossos and Phaestos were two important centers of this Bronze Age culture. About 1600 BC, the Mycenaean civilization developed on the mainland. Important Mycenaean centers were Athens and Thebes. A third, Cycladic, culture developed on the Cycladic Islands near Greece.

Aegean arts

Aegean architecture was large and impressive and consisted of palaces and fortifications. The Minoans were artistic people who excelled at fresco painting and painting on pottery. Popular subjects were landscapes and animals. The Mycenaeans produced a number of excellent sculptural objects like plaques, statuettes, containers, and masks in stone, metal, and ivory. Both cultures developed their own written language and all three had elaborate burial rituals and graves filled with beautiful metal and stone objects. By about 1450 BC, the Mycenaeans destroyed the Minoan culture and by 1200 BC, they were themselves destroyed by invading Dorians.

City-states

Following the Dorian invasion were the Dark Ages, or a period of chaos. Around 800 BC, the ancient Greek civilization began. As the civilization grew and the culture developed, colonies had to be formed in other countries to accommodate the growing population. Ancient Greece was divided into several self-governed city-states, the most important of which were Athens, Sparta, Corinth, and Thebes.

By the 5th century BC, Athens became the most important, powerful, and rich city-state. Democracy—a system in which governments are elected by the citizens of a country—was first introduced in Athens.

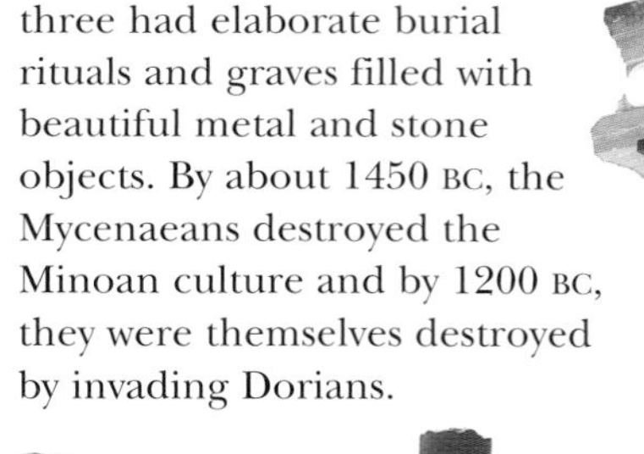

▾ The best of Minoan
The Palace of Knossos had a rectangular courtyard with four wings, which was characteristic of Minoan architecture. The wings consisted of the royal residence, workshops, a temple, banquet halls, throne room, a theater, and storerooms.

An Athenian tribute
The Parthenon is the most famous building of ancient Greece. It stands on a citadel atop a hill in Athens. It was a temple to Athena, the Greek goddess of war and wisdom.

Art and sports

The written language of the Mycenaeans was forgotten during the Dark Ages, so the Greeks had to make a new language using the Phoenician alphabets. Ancient Greeks were artistic people and the arts of sculpture, pottery, architecture and painting blossomed during this period. The art and literature of this period is so exceptional that it inspires people even today. Greek poets and playwrights, including Homer and Aristophanes, have written some of the greatest literary classics.

Peloponnesian War

When Athens became powerful around the 5th century BC, the Athenians began to dominate the other city-states. The city of Sparta grew jealous and, supported by Corinth, rose against Athens in 431 BC. The Peloponnesian War lasted for 27 years. At the end of the war, Athens was defeated and stripped of its powers.

▼ **Ancient athletes**
The ancient Olympic Games were held at Olympia very four years in honor of the king of Greek gods, Zeus. The first one took place in 776 BC.

▲ **A great mind**
Aristotle was an ancient Greek philosopher who also made valuable contributions to politics, astronomy, medicine, geography, and literature.

Try these too:

Ancient Rome (p 14–15),
Ancient Architecture (p 16–17),
The Renaissance (p 26–27)

Ancient Rome

The Roman civilization was the most powerful and widespread of all the ancient civilizations. At its peak, the empire stretched right across Western Europe, the northernmost parts of Africa, and the Middle East.

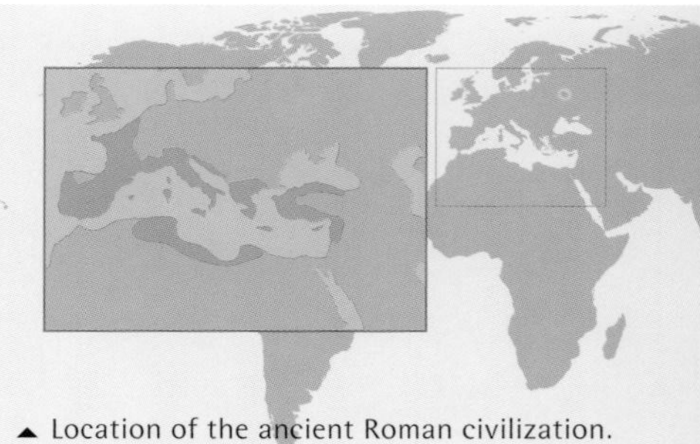

▲ Location of the ancient Roman civilization.

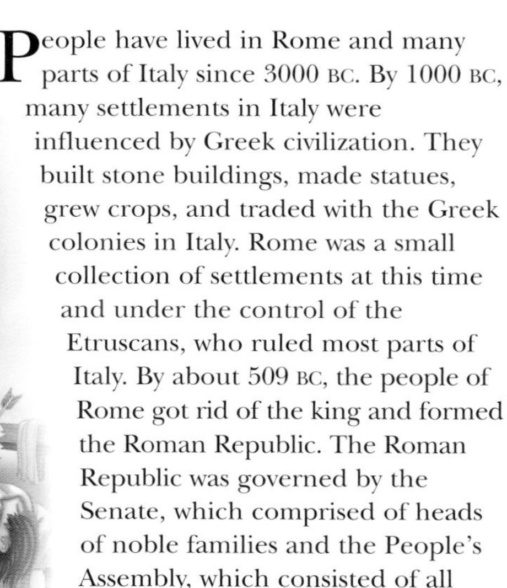

▲ **Military leader**
Julius Caesar was a great military leader and statesman.

People have lived in Rome and many parts of Italy since 3000 BC. By 1000 BC, many settlements in Italy were influenced by Greek civilization. They built stone buildings, made statues, grew crops, and traded with the Greek colonies in Italy. Rome was a small collection of settlements at this time and under the control of the Etruscans, who ruled most parts of Italy. By about 509 BC, the people of Rome got rid of the king and formed the Roman Republic. The Roman Republic was governed by the Senate, which comprised of heads of noble families and the People's Assembly, which consisted of all male citizens of Rome. Around 23 BC, Octavian ended the Republic and established the Roman Empire. He took the title of Augustus Caesar and brought order and peace to the chaotic Roman realm. The Romans ruled their vast empire until AD 476, when it crumbled due to weak kings and invasions by northern barbarians.

▶ **The legend of Rome**
According to legend, Romulus and Remus were the twin sons of Mars. They were abandoned as babies and a she-wolf nursed them. The twins were then adopted by a shepherd and, in 753 BC, Romulus founded the city of Rome at the spot where the shepherd had found him and his brother. The statue of the she-wolf and the babies is the symbol of Rome even today.

▼ **The great Roman**
Julius Caesar symbolized the rise of Rome more than any other Roman ruler. The great military leader and politician was responsible for extending the boundaries of the Roman Empire until it became the sole superpower in the region. Although Julius Caesar was the dictator of Rome, he never adopted the title of Emperor. However, he effectively destroyed the republic and set the foundation for a monarchy.

Pont du Gard

The Pont du Gard is an ancient Roman aqueduct in France. It was built in 19 BC, across the river Gardon. This three-tiered aqueduct has a road on the first level and a channel carrying water on the top level. It was part of a 31-mile (50-kilometer) long aqueduct that carried water from natural springs into the Roman town of Nîmes. This 161-foot (49-meter) tall structure, made of huge blocks of unplastered stone, has survived the ravages of time and has stood almost intact for over two thousand years.

ultural and artistic achievements

uring the Roman Republic and the Empire, t, architecture, and literature flourished. luch of it was inspired by ancient Greek ulture and later also by the cultures of other reas that were brought under Roman rule. he Romans were excellent engineers. They nproved roads and built public buildings in nany parts of their empire. Grand palaces, ublic bathhouses, triumphal arches, mphitheaters, and aqueducts (which carried ater over long distances) were some of the nost well-known public constructions. The evelopment of the dome and the arch during nis period truly revolutionized architecture. oman sculptures were true to life and closely esembled real people. The Romans made nural paintings, glass vessels, metal art, mosaics, and pottery. They also made statues, busts, and carved panels to decorate their buildings and arches, in marble, bronze, gold, and silver. The period between the 1st century BC and the middle of the 1st century AD is considered to be the golden age of Latin literature. Numerous poems, essays, historical accounts, and plays were written during this time. The ancient Roman style was a great source of inspiration for the art, architecture, and literature of the Middle Ages, Renaissance period, and even of the modern world. Ancient Romans were also keen sportsmen. They enjoyed running races, boxing, chariot racing, wrestling, swimming, hunting, ball games, and board games. Amphitheaters, especially used for gladiatorial games, and stadiums were common all over the empire.

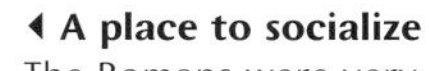

◂ A place to socialize
The Romans were very particular about keeping clean. Therefore, they built elaborate public bathhouses in every town. Ancient Roman bathhouses were not intended only for taking baths. People came to bathhouses to meet friends and business associates. Apart from bathing areas, many bathhouses also had a gymnasium, a library, and a games court.

Try these too:

Ancient Greece (p 12–13), Ancient Architecture (p 16–17), Europe in the Middle Ages (p 20–21), The Renaissance (p 26–27)

Key facts:

- The ancient Romans wore long pieces of woolen cloth called togas. Togas were draped in a stylish manner, but they were not convenient or comfortable. Later, influenced by the Greeks and Egyptians, they began wearing loose linen tunics. On special occasions they wore the toga over the tunic.
- The Romans built large and magnificent public bathhouses all over their empire. These bathhouses were more like leisure centers, and many of them boasted a library and a gym, as well as warm, hot, and cold baths and massage rooms. The bathers were also provided with entertainment, food, and drinks.
- Most Romans were poor, but those who were rich believed it was important to show off their wealth. They bought slaves to work for them. Slaves did housework, carried their masters in litters when they went out, ran errands, stood guard, and performed any other duties required of them, in return for food, clothes, and a place to stay.
- Latin was the widely accepted language of ancient Rome. It was derived from Greek and served as the official and scientific language in the Western world until the 18th century. Spanish, Romanian, Portuguese, French, and Italian, as well as many words in English, are derived from Latin.

Ancient Architecture

Architecture and building technology date back to when man first began settling down and living in houses. Buildings are often considered as status symbols that declare the power and position of their owners. A great deal of ancient architecture and some of the grandest buildings ever built were religious structures, such as temples and churches. Palaces and tombs are also grand and important structures of the ancient world.

Key facts:

- Medieval homes were timber framed. The timber was pegged together and fixed with braces to form the frame. The spaces between the pieces of timber were filled with wattle-and-daub. Rubble or brick and plaster was applied over the filling to even it out. The upper floors of some houses were 'jettied' out—they projected, so that more space was created.
- The Babylonians used clay to cement their bricks and the Egyptians used lime and gypsum. The Romans used a substance that was very similar to modern concrete. It was made by mixing volcanic ash with lime obtained from burning limestone.
- Two types of floor plan were used in medieval churches. They were the Latin cross and the Greek cross. The Latin cross plan looks like a crucifix. The altar in this plan is located at the far end. The Greek cross plan looks like a plus sign—it has four equal arms. The altar in this type is situated at the center, where the arms intersect.

In the Neolithic period, or Stone Age, buildings were made of rough stone boulders and covered with thatched roofs. Remains of such structures have been discovered at Skara Brae in Orkney, Scotland. In warmer areas, buildings had walls made from the bark of trees and woven grass or wattle-and-daub (woven mats plastered with mud). In the advanced civilizations of Mesopotamia, Egypt, the Indus Valley, and China, sun-dried mud bricks were used. Rich people used kiln-fired mud bricks as they were stronger.

The pyramids and temples of Egypt are among the most amazing surviving buildings of the ancient world. These enormous structures were precisely constructed from huge blocks of hand-cut stone, many of which are beautifully carved.

Classical style

Ancient Greek and Roman buildings were designed in what is now called the classical style. Examples of early buildings and domestic architecture have not survived in Greece because they were made using easily perishable materials like wood and mud bricks.

▲ **Monumental glory**
The Abu Simbel temple near Aswan in Egypt is guarded by massive rock-cut statues of the pharaoh, Ramses II.

Greek temples, on the other hand, were grand and beautiful structures made of limestone blocks decorated with carved marbl panels and statues. Some of the grandest buildings, like the Parthenon in Athens, were built entirely from marble. Most Greek buildings were square or rectangular in shape surrounded by columns, and had a front and back "porch." The roofs of these buildings were made of wooden beams covered with terracotta, or sometimes marble, tiles.

The Romans copied the Greek style, but improved it with some of their own innovations. They developed the use of the true arch and the dome. These were extremely important developments in the history of architecture. The Greeks, as well as the Romans, liked to decorate their buildings. They made carvings on pillars and walls and used lots of free-standing statues.

▼ **The pyramids at Giza**
The three most famous pyramids are at Giza near Cairo. The Great Pyramid, built about 2600 BC by the Pharaoh Khufu, is 450 feet (137 meters) high.

[M]edieval style

[B]y the Middle Ages, Christianity had spread [t]o most parts of Europe. This meant that [m]any new churches had to be built. The [t]wo main building styles of the medieval [p]eriod were the Romanesque and the Gothic. [M]edieval churches were tall, soaring [st]ructures with pointed-arch windows and [d]oorways. Gothic churches had a special [f]eature called 'flying buttresses'. These were [a]dditional supporting structures that were [b]uilt along the outer walls of the building. [G]othic churches also had beautiful stained-[gl]ass windows (made from pieces of colored [gl]ass), which illustrated stories from the Bible. [D]urham Cathedral in England and the [C]athedral of Pisa in Italy are Romanesque [c]athedrals that exist even today, while [S]alisbury Cathedral in England and Notre [D]ame de Paris, in France, are outstanding [e]xamples of Gothic religious architecture.

The other important structures built during [th]e medieval period were castles and fortified [w]alls. Immense stone castles were built to [p]rotect their lordly owners during [th]is time of war and violence, and many [re]main well preserved, for example, the Tower [o]f London and Windsor Castle in England.

[R]enaissance

[R]enaissance architecture returned to the [cl]assical style of graceful columns, domes, and [p]erfectly proportioned geometric buildings. [T]he style began in Italy and was popularized [b]y great architects like Brunelleschi, [B]ramante and Michelangelo. The Santa [M]aria del Fiore in Florence and St Peter's [B]asilica in Rome are two outstanding [e]xamples of Italian Renaissance architecture. [In] England, the style was a mixture of the old [G]othic and new European styles from France, [It]aly and Flanders. This was called the [E]lizabethan style of architecture, known for [it]s use of round arches, pillars, and domes as [w]ell as gabled turrets (small towers with [sl]oping roofs), mullioned windows (windows [w]ith vertical divisions in wood or stone), and [d]ecorative designs like scrolls and lozenges [(f]our-sided, elongated diamondlike shapes).

▲ **Stonehenge**
Stonehenge in Wiltshire, England, is widely considered to be the most famous prehistoric standing-stone monument in Europe. It is believed that it was built between 3000 and 1500 BC. It consists of several tall standing stones, or megaliths, set in a circle. These are surrounded by a ditch and a raised earthen circle.

Pantheon

The Pantheon in Rome was built around 27–25 BC by the Roman consul Marcus Agrippa. It was originally built as a temple to seven Roman gods who represented seven planets. In the 7th century AD the Pantheon was converted into a church. Most of the building was destroyed in a fire in AD 80, but the dome survived intact. The Pantheon is probably the oldest important building that has been continuously used since it was first constructed.

Some of the most important Renaissance buildings in England were designed by the well-known architect, Inigo Jones. The Queen's House at Greenwich and the Banqueting Hall in Whitehall, London, are two of his best-known designs.

Try these too:

Ancient Mesopotamia and Egypt (p 8–9), Ancient Greece (p 10–11)

▼ **Notre Dame**
This famous gothic cathedral in Paris was completed in 1345.

The Native Americans

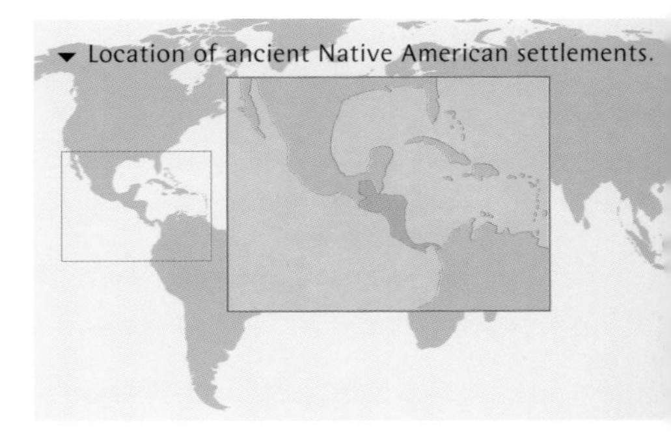
▼ Location of ancient Native American settlements.

The very first American people lived nearly 11,500 years ago. They are said to have come from northeastern Asia, across the Bering land bridge, which once connected America and Asia. These early people did not stay anywhere permanently—they hunted and gathered food on the move. Slowly they began settling down and living together in farming villages.

Key facts:

- Most Native American farmers and craftsmen lived in villages, in small houses. Some had just one room, while others had two or more tiny rooms. These houses were made of poles and thatch in warm areas or with wattle-and-daub, that is, clay plastered over mats made of twigs.
- Today, there are over 500 Native American tribes recognized by the United States government and many lesser-known tribes. The most well-known tribes are Cherokee, Navajo, Choctaw, Sioux, Apache, Blackfoot, Pueblo, Chippewa, Iroquois, and the Inuit.

Early Mississippians settled in present-day Illinois, Wisconsin, Indiana, and Kentucky around AD 900. They grew maize, made pottery, and traded with people in other parts of the continent. They lived in villages ruled by a chief, who was the most powerful person. The rest of the villagers were powerless and divided into different social classes. These people made large mounds or platforms, which were probably religious. Other native communities included a number of small tribes, collectively called Apache Indians, who lived in parts of Arizona and Mexico. Some groups settled down and cultivated crops, but others were fierce warrior nomads who lived in tents and hunted for food. The Inuit of Alaska and Canada form another group of Native Americans. These people were hunters and fishermen who ate whales, walruses, polar bears, and musk ox. They also used the skin and bones of these animals to make boats, sledges, tools, clothes, and even homes.

▲ **The mound-builders**
Mississippian mounds were usually square, rectangular or circular in shape. Temples, houses, and even burial sites were built on these mounds.

▼ **Riding on ice**
Traditionally the Inuit people traveled on the komatik, a low-slung sledge pulled by special sledge dogs called huskies. The person sat or lay down on this type of sledge. These sledges were made from the skin of seals or walruses. Today, however, the Inuit prefer to use snowmobiles to get from one place to another. Sledges are usually reserved for hunting and racing.

Native American clothing

The dressing style of the Native Americans depended on the climate of the place in which they lived. For instance, men in Central America wore only a cotton loincloth and women wore a dress made with a single piece of cloth, which had holes cut out for the head and hands. In some tribes, women wore belts or long blouses over this dress. In the colder parts of South America, like the Andes, woolen dresses and capes were also worn, and men wore shirts, kilts, and capes. The Inuit wore animal-skin clothes, parkas, and boots.

▲ A remarkable victory
ne Battle of the Little Bighorn (June 25–26, 1876) was n important battle in the Indian Wars. It was a battle etween the combined forces of Lakota and Northern heyenne tribes and the United States army. The tribal orces won the battle, fought on the banks of the Little ighorn River in eastern Montana.

nvasion of the native lands

'he Native Americans lived peacefully in ieir new land for several centuries until ie arrival of the Europeans. At first, the atives welcomed the foreigners. However, iey soon turned hostile when they realized iat the newcomers were there to stay. The atives were also unhappy with the Europeans s they did not respect their native culture nd way of life.

This led to a series of armed conflicts between the two parties. Known as the Indian Wars, these conflicts began in the early 1600s. Some of the worst battles, however, occurred after the United States had won its freedom from colonial rule. The white settlers forcibly relocated Native Americans in places far away from their homes as a means of gaining more territories for themselves. One of the worst incidents took place in 1838 when a huge population of Cherokee Indians were removed from their lands. About 4,000 Cherokees died during the relocation due to exhaustion and diseases.

A rich culture

Each Native American tribe has its own unique customs, traditions, language, and dress. However, some elements are common among all tribes. The ancestors of all modern tribes were nomads who hunted large animals like bison with bows and arrows. Early native settlers were good at pottery, painting, jewelry making, carving and weaving. Most Native American tribes also share religious beliefs and ceremonies. Shamanism was a major part of their life. Shamans were priests who were believed to be able to mediate between humans and the spirit world. They were also regarded as healers and guardians of the tribes. Most religious ceremonies are accompanied by chanting, beating of drums, and dancing.

▲ Totem pole
Native Americans believed that each tribe or individual was protected by an animal, a plant, or supernatural object or being. They called this object or being a totem.You could not choose your totem—it chose you. The Native Americans carved the images of their totems onto poles and displayed them near their houses or on graves.

▲ Traveling on water
In ancient times, Native Americans used a canoe called a dugout. A dugout was built by scraping out excess wood from the middle of a log of suitable size. The two ends of the boat were then sharpened to make the boat faster.

Try these too:

The Incas and Aztecs (p 130–131),
The Age of Exploration (p 134–135)

Europe in the Middle Ages

The term Middle Ages refers to the period between approximately AD 500 and AD 1500. It was a period of great changes in Europe. The Roman Empire had become too large and unmanageable to be ruled by one person. Many of the later emperors were weak and helpless against attacks from hostile neighboring tribes. The western part of the Empire collapsed in 476 AD and its provinces formed into separate kingdoms. It was a period of continual warfare, bloodshed, and power struggles.

Key facts:

- Serfs paid rent in the form of livestock, such as sheep, goats, pigs, and hens, or in the form of eggs, firewood, or wine. The lord of the manor decided how much each peasant had to pay.
- In 312 AD, the Roman emperor Constantine converted to Christianity and soon after it was declared the official religion of the Roman Empire. It was only after this that Christianity began to be accepted widely.
- Medieval craftsmen and traders were members of guilds, or associations. Each guild was responsible for setting rules, standards, and prices for the products produced by their members. This ensured fairness and equality. It also assured the traders of a fixed price and safeguarded them in times of hardship.
- In 1348, Europe was struck by the Black Death, or plague. This terrible disease originated in East Asia, and arrived first in Italy. Over the next three years, it spread right through the continent, killing millions of people.

One of the most significant changes of this period was the spread of Christianity. A number of monasteries were built and these became centers of power and wealth. People were encouraged, sometimes forced, to convert to Christianity, and Sunday mass was made compulsory.

Feudalism

By the Middle Ages, Western Europe consisted of several small kingdoms that were constantly at war with each other. Kings gifted large areas of land, called fiefs, to important people like barons and bishops. These barons and bishops, in return, provided the royal army with soldiers from their lands. With no single powerful ruler to protect the citizens, landlords soon became the most powerful people. They lived in manors, which usually consisted of a castle, a church, a village, and fields. The peasants, or serfs, who worked in the fields were the poorest people. They had to pay rent to the lord and serve him.

Europe during the Middle Ages.

The Crusades

At the end of the 11th century, Islamic Turks attacked the eastern part of the Roman Empire. The pope sent a huge army of Christians from Rome to fight against these Muslim invaders. This was the first of many Crusades, or Holy Wars. Several more were fought between the people of these two faiths over a period of 300 years. Another important war that decided the future of Europe was the Hundred Years War (1337–1453) between France and England.

◂ **The men of chivalry** The kings were served and protected by knights. These knights were young and brave warriors who were trained in warfare. Many of them fought for their kings in the Crusades. Some knights were monks, and they belonged to monasteries.

Medieval castles

The most imposing structures of the Middle Ages were castles. These large stone houses were built by barons and feudal lords to proclaim their wealth and power. Castles doubled up as fortresses within which their owners could hide, or from where they could launch an attack. Warwick Castle in England and Krak des Chevaliers in modern Syria are magnificent examples.

Vikings of Scandinavia

During the Middle Ages, Europe was attacked by brave and adventurous people from the north, south, and east. The Vikings of Scandinavia were the most influential among these. They attacked Ireland, England, and even Iceland. They were driven out of England by King Alfred the Great, only to return after his death. They also settled in France, and eventually their kingdoms in the north joined Europe.

Walls of protection
The earliest castles were made of wood and earth. As the hostilities between various European countries grew, castles began to be built of stone. They were further fortified with moats, drawbridges, and portcullises.

Rule of monarchs

The first major royal dynasty to rule over large parts of Europe was the Merovingians. They ruled over France, Belgium, Switzerland, and parts of Germany and they laid the foundations for modern Europe. They were followed by the Carolingians from Austria. During their rule, several schools and universities were founded, the Catholic Church became more powerful, and cities and towns grew. After the Carolingians lost power, the three most important centers in Europe were Britain, France, and Germany. These countries were ruled by a succession of dynasties, one sometimes taking over another.

Church art

Medieval churches were large and awe-inspiring buildings. They had arched doors and windows with stunning stained glass panels. Their inner walls were decorated with paintings of scenes from the Bible or other Christian themes. The churches also had carved pillars, relief panels, and statues. Many churches, monasteries, and wealthy people also commissioned illuminated manuscripts. These were beautifully illustrated scrolls or books on Christian themes.

A religious ruler
Charlemagne was the most popular Carolingian ruler. He was the king of Franks and Lombards, and the founder of the Holy Roman Empire. He was also a devout Catholic and had close relations with the pope. It was the pope who crowned Charlemagne emperor of the Holy Roman Empire.

Try these too:

Ancient Greece (p 12–13),
Ancient Rome (p 14–15),
Ancient Architecture (p 16–17),
Medieval Asia (p 22–23),
The Renaissance (p 26–27),
The Age of Exploration (p 28–29)

Powerful influence
The Crusades united major European powers under the Church, exposed the West to Middle Eastern culture, and marked the beginning of the Renaissance period.

Medieval Asia

At the same time as Europe was being established, India, China, Japan, and the Arabian countries were also going through a period of tremendous change and development. World religions like Christianity, Islam, Hinduism, and Buddhism were becoming widespread. Scientific inventions and artistic, cultural, and political developments laid the foundations of the modern world.

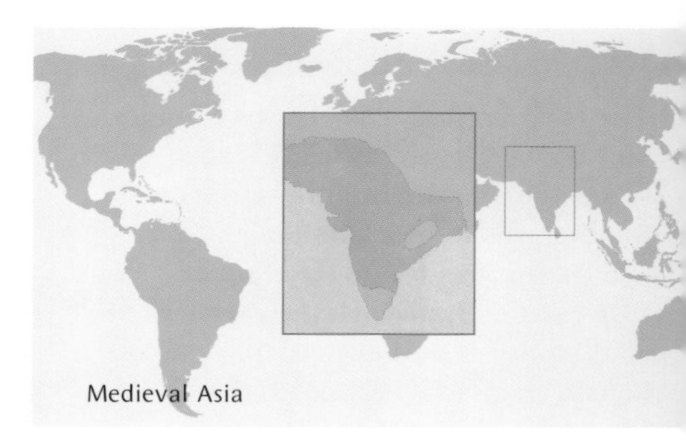

Medieval Asia

Key facts:

- Around the end of the 13th century AD, the Venetian traveler Marco Polo published a book about his travels along the Silk Road, the trade route between China and the West. It was widely read by Europeans of that time and cartographers and mariners referred to it for information about Asia.
- During the Gupta period in India (320–480 AD), a surgeon called Sushruta wrote a book called the *Sushruta Samhita*. The book contains information about 300 types of surgery and 120 types of surgical instruments. Sushruta could perform a vast range of surgery. He could fit artificial limbs and he even conducted plastic surgery.
- The people of the medieval Islamic kingdoms were mostly known as fearsome fighters. However, they were also extremely creative people who could make beautiful art objects. They produced excellent gold and silver jewelry; candle stands and containers; glass containers; ceramics; stone carvings; and even astronomical instruments.

In China, the Han dynasty brought peace and order back to the country. At the same time that Jesus was preaching his message in the West, Buddhism was becoming popular in China. Many people converted to this new religion. Paper was also invented in China at this time. Artists of this period were inspired to make numerous paintings of Buddhist themes.

The Golden Age

China's 'golden period' occurred during the the T'ang dynasty, between 618 and 907 AD. Landscape painting, sculpture, pottery, poetry and music, calligraphy, and the manufacture of porcelain ware reached new heights. Also, the introduction of printing made it possible for books to be made in large quantities. Over the course of time, the Chinese invented several useful things including the compass, the seismograph (to measure earthquakes), the clock, and gunpowder.

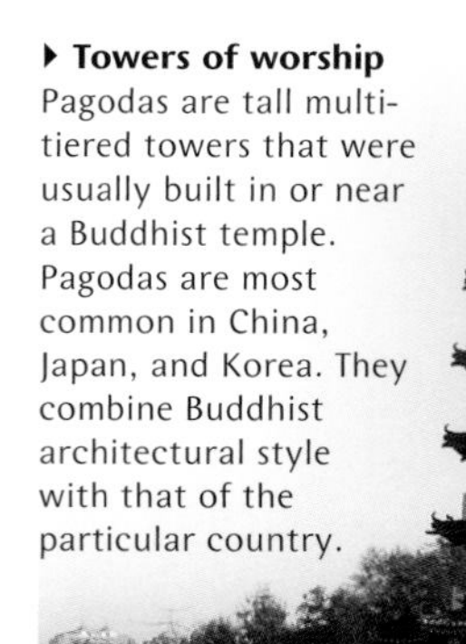

▸ Towers of worship
Pagodas are tall multi-tiered towers that were usually built in or near a Buddhist temple. Pagodas are most common in China, Japan, and Korea. They combine Buddhist architectural style with that of the particular country.

Mongolian power

In the 13th century, the Mongols were the most powerful people in Asia. Led by their king Genghis Khan (1162–1227), they brought China, Tibet, Burma, Iran, Eastern Europe, and parts of Russia under their control. Between 1251 and 1259, Genghis Khan's grandson Kublai Khan carried his grandfather's legacy forward and led a series of campaigns against China. In 1279, Kublai Khan gained control of China and became the first ruler of the Chinese Yüan dynasty.

Japan

The Japanese civilization developed later than those of its neighbors. It was only in 405 AD that Japan adopted a written language and even then they developed a writing system based on Chinese alphabets. In 600, Buddhism spread among the Japanese. Around this time, the Yamato dynasty ruled Japan, but the real power was in the hands of the shoguns, or military generals. By the 12th century, the Yamato emperors had lost all their power. The shoguns and their powerful families, called daimyos, took over.

Ajanta

In a deep ravine in western India, there are about 30 caves. Most of these caves—in Ajanta—were used as monasteries by Buddhist monks, while the rest were prayer halls. The monasteries are called *viharas.* They have a pillared verandah, a hall and several dormitories cut into the rock. The caves used as prayer halls are called *chaitya grihas.* These are long halls cut deep into the rock. The caves are decorated with beautiful carvings and some of them have paintings, too. The caves were built in two phases. The first ones were made some time in the second century BC, while the rest were carved between the fifth and sixth centuries AD.

ndia

'he Mauryan Empire, established by 'handragupta Maurya, dominated northern ndia in the 3rd century BC. Chandragupta nd his grandson Ashoka were the two reat rulers of this period. At the height f Mauryan power, the kingdom covered nost parts of India and Pakistan, and parts f Afghanistan.

cultural expansion

fter a brief period of instability, North ndia came under the control of the Gupta 'mpire in AD 320. Under the new rulers, art, cience, architecture, and literature flourished. 3ooks were written about medicine, surgery, stronomy, and mathematics.

At the same time, in South India, smaller kingdoms like the Pallavas, Cholas, and Chalukyas were also expanding and producing beautiful temples, palaces, sculptures and paintings.

Rise of the Mughals

From the late 12th century, for more than 300 years, India was ruled by a series of Muslim kings from West Asia. The last Muslim kingdom of the Lodhi dynasty ended with the arrival of Babur, the founder of the Mughal dynasty. The Mughals ruled India for more than 200 years.

The Islamic World

After the fall of the Roman Empire in the Middle East, the next major event that took place in this region was the birth of Islam in the 7th century AD. The Muslims of Arabia soon took over the surrounding areas of Palestine, Egypt, Mesopotamia, Syria, and Persia. From the 11th century onward, the Middle East was ruled by various Muslim kingdoms like the Seljuk Turks, the Mameluks, and the Ottoman Turks. These kingdoms terrorized Eastern Europe and blocked all land routes between Asia and Europe.

▲ **Towering above all**
The Qutub Minar in Delhi, the capital of India, is a great example of Mughal architecture. The minaret was built by the Muslim ruler, Qutub-ud-din-Aibak and his successors. This five-storied tower is made of red sandstone and has verses from the *Qur'an* carved on it.

◀ **A marvel in stone**
Mahabalipuram, a seaport town during the rule of the Pallava dynasty, is full of rock-cut temples. The beautiful Shore Temple was built in honor of the Hindu god, Shiva.

Try these too:

Ancient Mesopotamia and Egypt (p 8–9), Ancient India and China (p 10–11), Europe in the Middle Ages (p 20–21), The Age of Exploration (p 134–135)

The Incas and Aztecs

The Incas and Aztecs were the two most powerful and important Native American kingdoms between AD 1400–1600. Around 1438, the South American Quechua tribe formed the Inca Empire in the Andes, with their capital at Cuzco, in Peru.

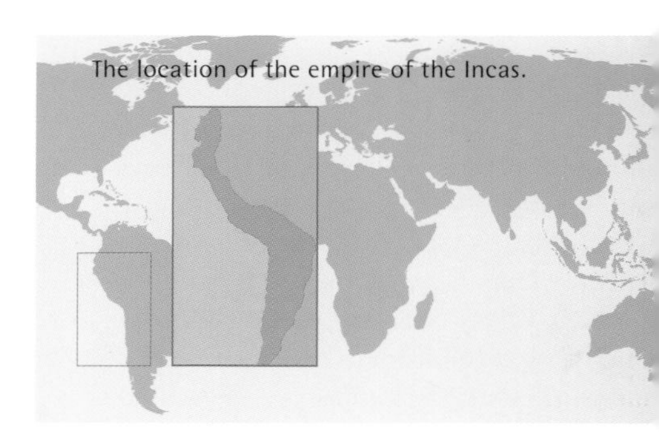

Key facts:

- The Quechua people called their kingdom Tawantinsuyu, or the "land of four quarters." This was because the Inca kingdom was divided into four parts, each under a governor.
- The Incas often moved large groups of people from one place to another within the empire. This was because, sometimes, a large number of people were needed to farm a particular area or to mine it. Large groups of Quechua people were also moved to newly conquered areas to prevent the local tribes from revolting against the Incas.
- The people of Tenochtitlán used hollowed logs made into boats to go up and down the canals in the city. Tenochtitlán was an island in a lake that was connected to the mainland by three raised roads. Aqueducts brought drinking water into the city.
- The Aztecs used the maguey, or agave, plant for many things. The spikes on the plant were used as needles, the leaves were used to make thatched roofs, the fiber was used to make rope, and the sap was used to make a drink called *pulque*.

The Incas conquered neighboring kingdoms and tribes and made them part of the Inca Empire. At the height of Inca power, the kingdom covered parts of present-day Argentina, Chile, Peru, Bolivia, and Ecuador. The Incas collected tax from all the tribes that they conquered. The tax was paid in the form of labor. Taxpayers had to work on Inca building projects, such as making mountain roads, tunnels, bridges, forts, and terraces for farming. The Incas were skilled farmers. They grew corn, potatoes, chilli peppers, beans, squash, peanuts, cassava, and quinoa. They built channels to bring water high up into the mountains in case the rains failed them. The Incas used hand tools such as spades, clubs, hoes, sticks, and foot plows to dig, break, and move earth. They raised guinea pigs, dogs, and ducks for meat, as well as llamas and alpacas for their meat, wool, and dung (which was used as fuel). They also used llamas to transport goods.

Incas worshiped nature and believed in life after death. When a king died, his body was mummified and preserved. The people would regularly offer food to it and consult it whenever they had a problem. Ordinary people were also mummified and laid to rest in tombs, along with food and water. The arrival of Spanish conquerors in 1532 ended the Inca Empire. They killed Atahualpa, the Inca emperor, and defeated the Inca armies.

▼ The Lost City
Machu Picchu is a well-preserved Inca city near Cuzco, Peru. This extraordinary city is located high on the Andes mountain, more than 7,700 feet (2,300 meters) above sea level. This city is hidden so well that it remained unknown to the outside world until 1911 when Hiram Bingham, an American historian, stumbled upon the city's ruins. The city had a large palace, a huge courtyard, temples, and homes for the royal staff.

Aztecs

The Aztecs were Native Americans who ruled over present-day Mexico. In fact their capital city Tenochtitlán was at the site of present-day Mexico City. The Aztecs ruled between 1428 and 1521, until they lost their homes and power to Spanish settlers. They were warriors who conquered many neighboring kingdoms. Once a kingdom was conquered, its people had to pay tribute to the Aztec ruler, *Huey Tlatoani* (which meant Great Speaker). However, for a nation of warriors, they had surprisingly few weapons. Those that they had were made of stone, not metal.

An Aztec's life

The Aztecs did not have many agricultural tools either. They mostly used sticks to dig the soil and sow seeds. They had not discovered the wheel, so they had no carts. They also did not have any beasts of burden (llamas) like the Incas. However, they were good traders. They exchanged their pots, tools, baskets, cloth, jewelry, and lake salt for jaguar skins, feathers, cotton, and rubber from other kingdoms. The sun god (Huitzilopochtli), rain god (Tlaloc), and wind god (Quetzalcoatl) were the major Aztec gods. The Aztecs built huge temple complexes with big stepped pyramids for these gods. Human beings, especially slaves brought from conquered territories, were sacrificed regularly to please the gods.

Quipu

The Incas used brightly colored threads called quipus to keep accounts and records of people, land, gold, animals, and stored grain in their kingdom. Red threads were used to maintain army records, yellow threads for gold, and so on. The colored threads were strung from a horizontal thread at the top and each one was knotted in a special way to record numbers and quantities. The knots at the top stood for 10,000, the ones below for 1,000 and so on until they worked their way down to one.

▲ **Building bridges**
The Incas built strong suspension bridges across mountains. These bridges were constructed with rope made of plaited grass woven together.

Try these too:

The Native Americans (p 18–19),
The Age of Exploration (p 28–29)

▲ **The stone of creation**
The Aztec sun stone, often mistakenly called the calendar stone, is a huge carved stone dedicated to the sun god. The stone is about 12 feet (3.5 meters) in diameter and the colorful carvings are thought to depict the Aztec belief that the world went through four cycles of creation and destruction before the Aztecs came into existence.

▶ **Pipe smokers**
Smoking pipes was an important part of the Aztec culture. The Aztecs smoked pipes during social gatherings and even at religious ceremonies. Pipes used by the Aztec priests during rituals were often decorated with elaborate carvings.

The Renaissance

The Renaissance period marked the end of the Middle Ages and the beginning of a more modern world. It was a period of great cultural change in Europe. Artists and writers rediscovered the classical Roman and Greek styles of art and architecture, as well as ancient books and the Greek and Latin languages.

Key facts:

- Renaissance means "rebirth." The name was first used by the Italian historian Giorgio Vasari, who wrote about the *Rinascenza* that was taking place in Italy. The word was later translated into the French *Renaissance.*
- It was during the Renaissance period that artists regularly began signing their works. Artists began creating art to express themselves and they took pride in their work, unlike the anonymous artists of the Middle Ages.
- Cities and ports became very important during the Renaissance period. They were the centers of artistic activity and foreign trade. Banks became significant institutions as they provided money for businesses and earned huge profits.

The Renaissance period began in the 14th century AD in Italy, particularly in the city of Florence. In fact, the construction of the dome that tops the Santa Maria del Fiore Cathedral in Florence is widely regarded as the beginning of Renaissance architecture. The start of the Renaissance period itself is traced back to the Italian poet, Petrarch, who was in awe of ancient Roman literary works. By the 15th century, it had spread to other parts of Europe, including France, England, and Germany. The Florentines felt that the culture and style of the Middle Ages was barbaric, and looked back for inspiration to the classical styles of Greece and Rome. Their art, architecture, sculpture, and writing were heavily influenced by these ancient styles. Some of the greatest works of art were produced during the Italian Renaissance by artists such as Donatello, Michelangelo, Leonardo da Vinci, and Raphael, and architects such as Alberti and Brunelleschi.

Pietà
Michelangelo's Pietà is one of the finest Renaissance sculptures. This marble sculpture depicts the Virgin Mary holding the body of her son Jesus, after he was crucified. The sculpture can now be found in St. Peter's Basilica in Rome. The sculpture is regarded as one of Michelangelo's greatest works.

Santa Maria del Fiore
The dome of Santa Maria del Fiore cathedral in Florence is regarded as Filippo Brunelleschi's greatest work. Its high dome was built by laying bricks in a spiral pattern on an octagonal (eight-sided) base. It was the first of its kind.

Humanism

Humanism was the underlying philosophy behind the Renaissance. It emphasized the development of human virtues, such as compassion and honor; and human potential in the arts and sciences. Humanists wished to transform the ignorant society of the "dark ages" into a new, more enlightened culture. Their main source of inspiration was classical literature—the recently translated works of Greek and Roman philosophy, rhetoric, and history, which taught new ways of explaining the world, based on reason rather than religion. Many of the early humanists were also deeply Christian, but they disagreed with the way medieval Christianity ignored human development and focused purely on the spiritual. They believed that ordinary human activities, such as education, business, and the arts, were also very important. The rise of humanism coincided with social changes in Europe, especially the growth of commerce and the expansion of towns and cities. This would lead to the gradual transfer of political and economic power from the clergy and nobility to the wealthy city merchants and businessmen–the middle classes.

Printing press

In the early 15th century, a small-time German metalworker by the name Johann Gutenberg invented the printing press. The first book to be printed on his press was the Holy Bible. Gutenberg's invention revolutionized Western civilization. The mass production of printed books made information and knowledge much more easily available to everyone.

lizabethan England

he Renaissance in England is also known
the Elizabethan era, or the Shakespearean
ge. It was England's golden age of literature,
chitecture, science, and exploration.
In England, unlike in Italy, literature
ined more importance than the other
ts during the Renaissance. Poets such
Edmund Spenser and John Milton, and
aywrights like William Shakespeare and
hristopher Marlowe, wrote some of the
ost important English literature during
is period. The architecture of this period
oke away from the large, cold, and dark
edieval style. Elizabethan buildings had
gh ceilings and large windows and were
corated on the outside and the inside.

eformation

longside the spread of new ideas came
creasingly urgent calls for reform of the
hurch. People were critical of its wealth and
rceived corruption. Many of them decided
break away from the Roman Catholic
hurch and form Protestant religious groups,
ch as the Lutherans, Calvinists, and
ennonites. These groups had their own
aders and did not accept the pope as their
ligious head. In 1534, England became a
otestant country when King Henry VIII
clared himself head of a new Church of
ngland. By the end of the Middle Ages, the
a of the Church as a single, all-powerful
sititution, dominating every aspect of
ople's lives, and uniting Europe under the
thority of the pope, was over.

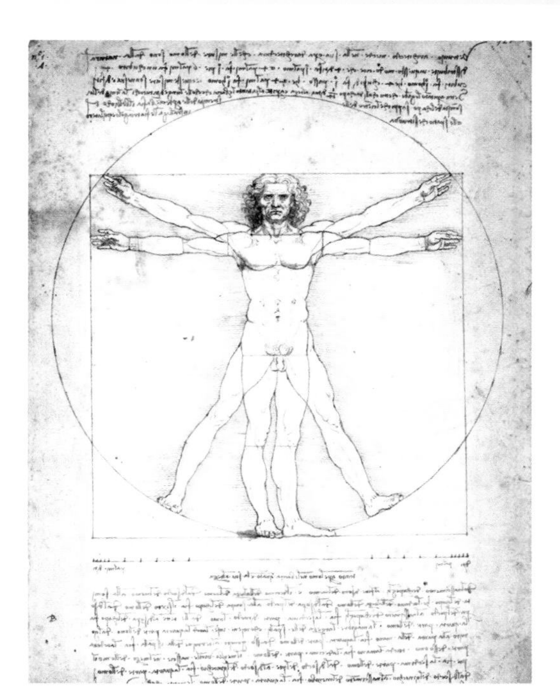

▼ Michelangelo's Original Sin
The ceiling of the Sistine Chapel in Rome was painted by Michelangelo. The ceiling contains scenes from the Book of Genesis, of which the Creation of Adam and the Original Sin are the best known.

▲ Reforming Christians
John Calvin was one of the most important religious reformers, who established the Protestant system of Calvinism.

◀ Renaissance man
Leonardo da Vinci's Vitruvian Man is the most popular symbol of the Renaissance period.

Try these too:

Ancient Greece (p 12–13), Ancient Rome (p 14–15), Europe in the Middle Ages (p 20–21), Ancient Architecture (p 16–17)

The Age of Exploration

The period between the 15th and 17th centuries is commonly known as the Age of Exploration. During this time, European countries such as England, Spain, Portugal, France, Germany, and the Netherlands, sent out groups of people to explore the oceans and to find out what lay beyond them. Several adventurous merchants, navigators, and wealthy gentlemen led explorations for their countries or for their own personal gain.

Key facts:

- People have been traveling to foreign lands since about 3000 BC. The Egyptians, Mesopotamians, Indus Valley people, and Chinese traveled over land and sea to trade goods.
- Travel by land became difficult and unsafe due to the plague raging throughout Europe and because of the fierce Muslim kingdoms in the Middle East. By the 14th century, shipbuilding and mapmaking had developed considerably in Europe, so travel by sea was a safer choice.
- It was the Portuguese explorer Ferdinand Magellan who gave the Pacific Ocean its name, which was derived from the Spanish word *pacifico*, meaning "peaceful"—because he found the ocean to be very calm.

The Portuguese were the first to begin exploring sea routes. They set out for Africa under the patronage of Prince Henry the Navigator. By 1434, they had landed on the west coast of Africa. More than 50 years later, Bartolomeu Dias rounded the southern tip of the continent, the Cape of Good Hope, paving the way for a sea route from Europe to India through the Indian Ocean. In 1497, Vasco da Gama sailed along the route Dias had discovered to reach India.

Spanish explorers

The sea routes to India and China, discovered by the Portuguese, were long and extremely dangerous. This prompted the Spanish navigator Christopher Columbus to head west in the hope of finding a quicker and safer way to these countries across the Atlantic Ocean. After traveling for over a month, Columbus landed on an island in the Caribbean Sea, in the present-day West Indies. Columbus thought it was an island close to Asia. He continued his journey and discovered Cuba, Haiti, and the Dominican Republic. Columbus was convinced that these new lands were the East Indies (lands to the east of India) and he named the natives 'Indians'. Between 1493 and 1502, Columbus made three more voyages. During these trips, he came upon more Caribbean islands, including Jamaica, Trinidad and Tobago, and Grenada. He also discovered Central America and Venezuela in South America.

◂ Undying faith
Christopher Columbus died on May 20, 1506, in Valladolid, Spain. Even on his death bed, Columbus was convinced that he had discovered a new sea route to Asia.

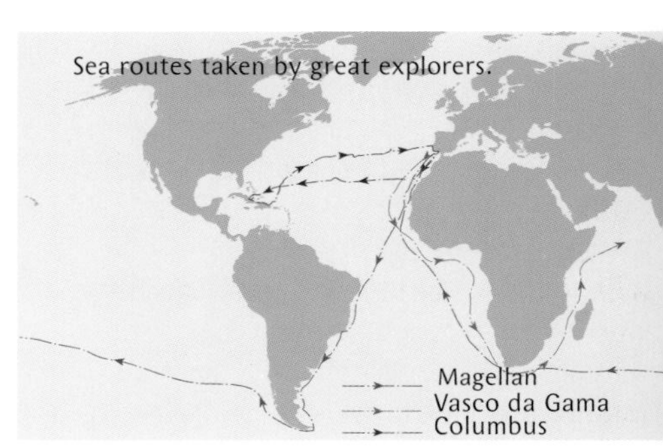

Ferdinand Magellan was a Portuguese explorer who sailed under the banners of bot Spain and Portugal. Supported by Charles I, the king of Spain, Magellan set out in 1519 to find a western route to the Spice Islands of the East. After stopping in South America for a few months in 1520, Magellan and his crew reached the Philippines in 1521. Magellan became involved in the rivalries between the natives and was killed by angry islanders. However, his crew eventually reached the Moluccas in Indonesia and one ship returned successfully to Spain in 1522. They were the first people to sail around the world.

▴ Amerigo Vespucci
Amerigo Vespucci was an Italian mapmaker and merchar who was the first to identify America as a new continent and not a part of the East. America was named after him

Viking pioneers

The Vikings of Scandinavia were the earliest seafaring people to cross the Atlantic Ocean. They discovered Iceland, Greenland, and Newfoundland, and sailed along the coast of Canada long before other European countries set out in search of new lands. During the period between 870 and 930, the Vikings settled in Iceland. In 930, the ruling chiefs established a parliament there. In 982, Eric the Red sailed from Iceland and discovered Greenland. Nearly 20 years later, his son Leif Eriksson discovered Newfoundland.

rench discoveries

rance was keen to explore the west and the rench mariner Jacques Cartier was the first to xplore the area along the St Lawrence River ı Canada. Samuel de Champlain and Sieur e La Salle followed Cartier's route a few years ıter. Champlain claimed Quebec for France ıd La Salle traveled down the Mississippi and laimed Louisiana.

English expeditions

John Cabot led the first English expedition west in order to find a shorter and safer route to the spice-producing countries of the East. In 1497, Cabot landed in Newfoundland, Canada. Between 1576 and 1578, Martin Frobisher made three voyages to Canada and claimed a large part of the new land for England.

The English navigator and mapmaker James Cook undertook three historic voyages between 1768 and 1779. On the first, he charted New Zealand and the east coast of Australia. On the second, he discovered several South Pacific islands and crossed the Antarctic Circle in search of Antarctica. On his last voyage, he discovered Hawaii and sailed north to Alaska. He was the first person to map the east coast of Australia.

Sir Francis Drake was one of the most famous English explorers. In 1580, he became the first Englishman to sail around the world. After passing through the Magellan Strait, a storm blew his ship so far south, he became the first explorer to cross the Antarctic Circle.

▲ Man of many talents
As well as a fearless explorer, James Cook was an accomplished cartographer who made maps of all the places he visited.

Try these too:

The Native Americans (p 18–19), Medieval Asia (p 22–23),
The Incas and the Aztecs (p 24–25)

◀ Sailing on
The galleon, the *Golden Hind*, was Sir Francis Drake's flagship on his voyage around the world. Galleons were large sailing ships with many decks, which were widely used in Europe between the 16th and 18th centuries. They were armed with cannons and used for both wars and exploration.

▲ Hernándo's mission
Hernándo Cortés was a Spanish conquistador who was famous for his conquest of the Aztec empire. Hearing about the immense wealth of the Aztecs, Cortés attacked Mexico in 1519. He conquered this region and claimed it for Spain in 1521 after defeating the Aztecs in battle.

Index